W9-AUM-491

CAN PEOPLE STOP BEING VIOLENT?

Kevin Cunningham

Mitchell Lane

PUBLISHERS

2001 SW 31st Avenue
Hallandale, FL 33009
www.mitchelllane.com

THINKING ALOUD

First Edition, 2020.
Author: Kevin Cunningham
Designer: Ed Morgan
Editor: Sharon F. Doorasamy

Series: Thinking Aloud
Title: Can People Stop Being Violent? / by Kevin Cunningham

Hallandale, FL : Mitchell Lane Publishers, [2020]

Library bound ISBN: 9781680203370
eBook ISBN: 9781680203387

Library of Congress Cataloging-in-Publication Data
Names: Cunningham, Kevin, 1966- author.
Title: Can people stop being violent? / by Kevin Cunningham.
Description: First edition. | Hallandale, FL : Mitchell Lane Publishers, 2019. | Series: Thinking aloud | Includes bibliographical references and index.
Identifiers: LCCN 2018028575| ISBN 9781680203370 (library bound) |
  ISBN 9781680203387 (ebook)
Subjects: LCSH: Violence—Juvenile literature.
Classification: LCC HM886 .C86 2019 | DDC 303.6—dc23
LC record available at https://lccn.loc.gov/2018028575

PHOTO CREDITS: Design Elements, freepik.com, p. 9 a hre.www.flaticon.com, p. 15 Arian Zwegers CC-BY-2.0, p. 20 shakko CC-BY-SA-3.0, p. 23 US Embassy Jerusalem CC-BY-2.0 Blues and Rock for Humanity. November 2017

Contents

CHAPTER 1
The Neverending Problem 4

CHAPTER 2
What We Are or What We Become 8

CHAPTER 3
A Giant Form of Violence 12

CHAPTER 4
Smash, Bam, Crunch, Ka-boom, Snikt! 16

CHAPTER 5
The Nonviolent Way 20

Prompts 24

Timeline 29

Glossary 30

Find Out More 31

Works Consulted 31

On the Internet 31

About the Author 32

Words in **bold** throughout can be found in the Glossary.

THE NEVERENDING PROBLEM

On February 14, 2018, Nikolas Cruz entered Marjory Stoneman Douglas High School in Parkland, Florida. Cruz carried a rifle inside a case. He began shooting into classrooms. To draw people out, he set off the fire alarm. Some students fled the building. Others hid. Trapped students sent texts to family. Cruz killed 14 students and three adults.

People rushed to explain what happened. Some blamed Cruz's problems with mental illness. Others criticized a deputy who stayed outside. Easy access to powerful guns also drew attention. "Guns give these disgusting people the ability to kill other human beings," tweeted Parkland student Carly Novell. "This IS about guns and this is about all the people who had their life abruptly ended because of guns."

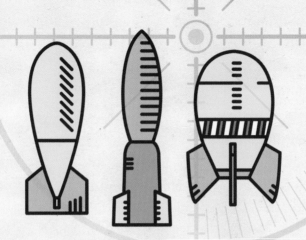

Crime. War. Torture. Violence fills the news. Still, many people consider violence a rare event. In fact, it occurs across everyday life.

Long ago, people committed violence with rocks and clubs. Today, someone at a computer may wipe out hundreds of people with a single drone. Guns, tanks, planes—all make it easy to kill humans by the tens of thousands every year. Tomorrow's robots and lasers will make it even easier. At the twist of a key, nuclear weapons could destroy the human race.

FREQUENT VICTIMS, FREQUENT SILENCE

Family violence affects women far more than men. In parts of India and Myanmar, people once encouraged a woman to burn herself alive when her husband died.

Chapter ONE

> # I AM BECOME DEATH, THE DESTROYER OF WORLDS.
> —*Bhagavad Gita*, quoted by J. Robert Oppenheimer at the first atomic bomb test

MANY FACES OF VIOLENCE

Violence goes beyond guns and fists. "Intolerance is itself a form of violence," said the Indian leader Mahatma Gandhi. **Civil rights** activist Julian Bond made a similar statement about poverty: "Violence is black children going to school for 12 years and receiving six years' worth of education."

Yet, despite the danger, violence never seems to go away. "Violence is like a weed," said Simon Wiesenthal. "It does not die even in the greatest drought."

Many holy books command followers not to kill. Yet humans kill. "The supreme art of war," said the Chinese philosopher Sun Tzu (545–470 BCE), "is to subdue the enemy without fighting." Yet war never ends.

Are we just born to hurt other living things? If violence is wrong, why do we keep doing it? Do humans learn violence? Or are we born that way? Can people stop? Philosophers and the rest of us struggle with these big questions.

Chinese philosopher
Sun Tzu

WHAT WE ARE OR WHAT WE BECOME

Thomas Hobbes (1588–1679) believed humans practiced "a restless desire for power after power." Like Hobbes, modern philosophers often look at how people use violence to fight for power. The two things seem to go hand in hand. Soldiers use powerful weapons to defeat an enemy, to take one example.

Hannah Arendt (1906–1975), however, saw power and violence as separate. Not only that, she believed they worked against each other. "Violence can destroy power," she said. "It is utterly incapable of creating it." Violence, she wrote, happens when people fear losing power, or when they have none at all.

> # MOTHERS ARE THE STRENGTH OF THE COUNTRY/ WITH A BRAVE HEART SHE SENDS HER CHILDREN/ TO THE BATTLEFIELD FAR AWAY.
>
> —"Haha no uta" (1943), Japanese schoolchildren song

Other thinkers have focused on the use of violence against certain groups. Simon de Beauvoir saw violence in the way men refused to let women be equal. "All **oppression** creates a state of war," she said. "There is no exception."

Malcolm X thought African Americans had to push back against oppression by white people. "I am not against using violence in self-defense," he said in a speech. "I don't even call it violence when it's in **self-defense**. I call it intelligence."

BEYOND SEVERE PUNISHMENT

Humans kill in strange ways. Some Asian rulers once used specially trained elephants to crush criminals. The Portuguese and British sometimes stretched a troublemaker across the mouth of a cannon—and fired the cannon. Persians, the Roman Catholic Church, and others walled up people in a tiny room, a punishment called immurement.

Chapter TWO

Professor Tsenay Serequeberhan stated that Europeans treated Africans so horribly that, for Africans, "Violence is not a choice." That is, European oppression was to blame for making violence a part of their daily lives.

Many thinkers see violence as a basic part of being human. According to Xun Kuang (c. 310–c. 230 BCE) "Human nature is evil, and goodness is [only] caused by intentional activity." Immanuel Kant said, "War seems to be ingrained in human nature, and even to be regarded as something noble to which man is inspired by his love of honor, without selfish motives."

In the past, many philosophers also worked as scientists. Both jobs involve trying to answer tough questions. Today's philosophers draw on science for ideas on the problem of violence.

GETTING THE LEAD OUT

Forty years ago, lead in gasoline polluted the air. Lead causes health problems. Research also suggests exposure to lead makes humans more violent. Governments began to ban lead in gas, paint, water pipes, and other products. In 2011, the United Nations said getting rid of leaded gas alone had saved more than 1 million lives.

Chimpanzees may offer us clues. In the 1970s, scientist Jane Goodall watched two chimpanzee groups fight a fierce war. Some took her work to mean that chimps, our closest ape relatives, practiced violence like our pre-human selves. David Carrier, a biologist, later led a team that measured human bodies. Carrier's work suggested nature shaped our hands to make a fist—humanity's first weapon.

Scientists, like philosophers, continue to disagree. Some think we learn violence. Others insist we're born that way. Experts call the argument **nurture versus nature**.

A Giant Form of Violence

The Polish-Jewish lawyer Raphael Lemkin (1900–1959) invented the word genocide in 1943. Genocide means killing people because they belong to a certain **ethnicity**, religion, social class, nation, or other group. As diplomat Samantha Power said, people committing genocide want to destroy a group "not because of anything they did but because of who they are."

Lemkin himself fled Germany's attempt to destroy Europe's Jewish population. Germany's government, under Nazi Party dictator Adolf Hitler, blamed the nation's problems on Jews. The Nazis organized a killing machine. They worked with the German military and nonmilitary Germans, Poles, French, and others. "Monsters exist," said Primo Levi. "[But] more dangerous are the common men . . . ready to believe and to act without asking questions."

GRAND PLANS, TERRIBLE IDEAS

Philip Gourevitch, a journalist, called genocide "an exercise in community building." A leader claims destroying another group will solve all problems. Killing the victims gives his followers a sense of togetherness. They also see themselves as an important part of the leader's plan. That's one reason why attackers often include everyday citizens.

Railroads and trucks took Jewish prisoners from across Europe to **concentration camps**. "When we arrived," Alice Lok Cahana recalled, "the dead were not carried away any more, you stepped over them, you fell over them if you couldn't walk." Guards killed Jews by starvation, hard labor, shooting, beating, exposure to cold weather, and with poison gas. Elsewhere, Germans and their helpers slaughtered Jews wherever they found them. Six million died in a genocide we now call the Holocaust. Only one of Raphael Lemkin's 50 relatives survived.

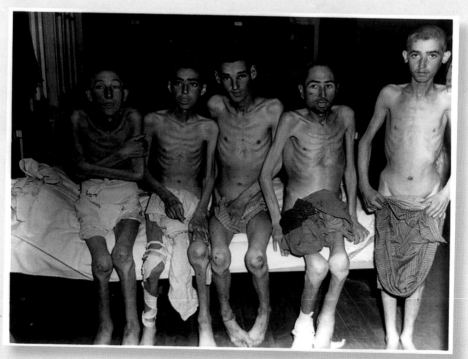

Five starving men in a German concentration camp at the time of liberation by the U.S. Army

The Holocaust followed other genocides. Lemkin studied Turkey's attempt to wipe out Armenians from 1915–1923. Germans first committed genocide in South-West Africa (today's Namibia) in 1904–1908. They drove the Nama and Herero people from their lands with violence and starvation.

Genocide against ethnic groups still happens. The Hutus of Rwanda massacred Tutsis and Pygmy Batwas in a 100-day period in 1994. The next year, Bosnian Serbs used concentration camps, executions, and mass murder against Bosnia's Croats and Muslims.

Governments can spark genocides to force citizens to go along with new ideas. The **communist** Soviet Union told Ukraine's rural people to move to massive farms in 1932–33. When the farmers refused, the government starved millions to death.

> MY SON WAS CLINGING TO MY DRESS. AN ARAB LOOKING MAN, IN A UNIFORM WITH MILITARY INSIGNIA, STOPPED HIS CAR NEXT TO ME. HE GRABBED MY SON FROM ME AND THREW HIM INTO A FIRE.
>
> —Kalima, a mother in a Darfur village, to the British Broadcasting Corporation

BLUE EYES VERSUS BROWN EYES

In 1970, schoolteacher Jane Elliott divided her class of third-graders into two groups. She favored children with blue eyes on the first day. On the second day, brown-eyed students received the special treatment. In each case, the students she treated unfairly felt ashamed, angry, and sad. They also performed worse on tests.

The Khmer Rouge believed all Cambodians should live on farms. They killed people with a college education, business owners, foreign language speakers, the religious, factory workers, non-Cambodians—anyone who didn't fit into their plan.

Sudan's genocide (2003–present) against the Fur, Zaghawa, and other peoples in Darfur had many causes. (Genocides always do.) The government wanted Darfuri's land for its allies. Officials encouraged old hatreds between Arabs, non-Arabs, and tribal groups.

The Bhuddist Stupa at Choeung Ek, Cambodia, that houses thousands of skulls of the victims from the Khmer Rouge regime in the 1970's.

CHAPTER FOUR

SMASH, BAM, CRUNCH, KA-BOOM, SNIKT!

It's a plain fact: humans find violence entertaining. That's always been true. In the 1800s, the Brothers Grimm wrote down old fairy tales filled with blood and murder. More than once, Japanese playwright Chikamtsu Monzaemon ended a show with deaths. William Shakespeare's *King Lear* kills off almost every main character.

Today's **popular culture** provides us with plenty of violent entertainment, too.

From Optimus Prime to Black Panther, action heroes dish out (and take) lots of punishment. *Deadpool* and *Logan* show superheroes that kill in brutal ways. The mega-violent *Wolf Warrior 2* became China's biggest moneymaker ever in 2017. Filmmakers have even learned a trick. Scientists know how long it takes for humans to lose concentration. Movie directors make sure to put in an action scene every so often to keep us hooked.

BLOOD SPORTS

Some entertainment features real killing. Gladiators fought each other or battled wild animals to thrill ancient Romans. In South Asia, forcing roosters to fight goes back thousands of years. Aztecs made prisoners of war battle five warriors to the death as a part of a public religious ceremony.

Police officers, detectives, even kid detectives—television without crime would be hours of blank screen. The cops on *CSI* solved gruesome murders for years. Reality TV like *48 Hours* goes into detail about real crimes. As for noncrime shows, the zombie drama *The Walking Dead* competes with *Game of Thrones* to kill more people.

Readers love violence and murder. Edgar Allen Poe invented the crime **genre** in the mid-1800s. Since then detectives like Sherlock Holmes have become household names. Crime novels also fill young adult fiction. *The Silence of Murder*, an award-winning book by Dandi Daley Mackall, revolves around a murder.

> # KILLING RIPS THE SOUL APART. IT'S A VIOLATION AGAINST NATURE.
>
> —J. K. Rowling, *Harry Potter and the Half-Blood Prince*

Many classic noncrime books offer violence. *The Chocolate War* ends with a horrific fight. Katniss in the *The Hunger Games* battles for her life again and again. A dictator attacks the rabbit heroes of *Watership Down*. In all these novels, powerful figures inflict violence on the main characters.

Video game violence sells. It also creates **controversy**. Government officials, educators, and parents' groups often point to the first-person shooter (FPS) genre as a problem. *The Call of Duty FPS* games take players into war. In *Far Cry 5*, the player plays a deputy given weapons to destroy a dangerous religious group. China, Malaysia, and some other countries regularly ban violent games.

THE PLAY WRITTEN AS WORLD WAR II BEGAN

Bertolt Brecht wrote *Mother Courage and Her Children* in 1939. Mother Courage makes her living by selling goods to an army. She doesn't stop even when war kills her three children one by one. "You don't want peace, you want war," one character says, "because you profit by it."

Violence is just as popular in music. "I shot a man in Reno," sang country legend Johnny Cash, "just to watch him die." For hundreds of years, people from Corsica to Georgia to India have sung about robbers and feuds. Traditional music in English-speaking countries includes an entire genre of murder ballads like Lead Belly's "In the Pines." The lyrics in Mexico's *narcocorrido* songs not only describe murders but use real events and people.

THE NONVIOLENT WAY

Thinkers have always offered alternatives to violence. "It is here that all the concerns of man go wrong, when they wish to cure evil with evil," said Sophocles (496–406 BCE). All of the major world religions teach some version of "Do to others what you would have them do to you."

Two ideas in particular have had a powerful influence: nonviolence and pacifism.

A believer in nonviolence never harms living creatures, including him- or herself. Nonviolent methods aim to change an opponent's mind. A nonviolent person works without anger. No insults. No threats. And, if someone insults or threatens you, you do nothing.

A bust of Sophocles

But the philosophy of nonviolence goes further. It states a person must work against oppression, poverty, and other evils. Martin Luther King Jr. (1929–1968) said: "Nonviolence is the answer to the crucial political and moral question of our time— the need for man to overcome oppression and violence without resorting to violence and oppression."

King struggled against racism and poverty in the United States. He drew on the work of Mahatma Gandhi (1869–1948). Gandhi worked to free India from rule by Great Britain. He called his nonviolent philosophy satyagraha, or truth force. "Satyagraha is a weapon of the strong," he warned. "It admits of no violence under any circumstance whatever; and it always insists upon truth."

Mahatma Gandhi

THE BATEK WAY

The Batek of Malaysia live by hunting and gathering. Individuals keep few possessions. Everyone shares food and land. Batek don't believe in violence. The people involved talk over a specific problem. If that fails, they ask the community for advice. If that fails, they move out of the community until the trouble passes.

Pacifism shares many ideas with nonviolence. Above all, a pacifist opposes violence. Some pacifists would say violence is always wrong. Others would allow violence in self-defense.

Pacifism doesn't teach that you must work for change. Many pacifists, however, have done so. Bertrand Russell, the British mathematician and pacifist, went to jail for protesting World War I. The Nazis killed college student Sophie Scholl after she passed out antiwar leaflets in Munich, Germany.

Scientific thinkers study nonviolence, too. The 1986 Seville Statement, signed by 20 researchers, stated humans were not born to commit violence. Douglas Fry, an expert on war and peace, listed 70 societies without war. In Western Australia, he found, some Martu people speak a language that doesn't have a word for *warfare*.

The Federal Bureau of Investigation says violent crimes in America fell by almost half from the early 1990s to 2016. We see fewer wars than in the past. Are more people exploring alternatives to violence? It's too soon to tell. All of us, not just philosophers, must keep searching for answers. It's worth it, to make people's lives safer and happier. One day, it may even save our species.

Daryl Davis

MEETING HATE WITH FRIENDSHIP

African American musician Daryl Davis convinced many people to leave the Ku Klux Klan, a racist group. How? He sat down to talk with them. "You will find that you both have something in common," he said. "You're forming a relationship and as you build about that relationship, you're forming a friendship."

LIFE, DEATH, AND THE RUNAWAY TROLLEY

It is easy to state we should always save a life. Philosophers, however, invent experiments that force us to think about life and death. Philippa Foot presented The Trolley Problem in 1967. The problem goes like this:

You see a trolley car racing toward five people tied to the railroad tracks. If you pull a switch, the train car will shift turn onto another set of tracks. But one person is tied to those tracks. Should you

1. not pull the switch and let the trolley kill the five people
or
2. pull the switch and let it kill one person?

Ask yourself questions about whether a person should or shouldn't pull the switch. Is it better to save more people? If a person does not pull the switch, is she responsible for what happens, since she did not create the problem? Is choosing to do nothing the same as doing something? Make a list of other questions that pop into your mind. Try not to focus on whether either decision is right or wrong.

Another Way of Saying It

Slang refers to words we use to replace more specific, older words. We invent slang to add color to language. Often it sounds cool or funny. We also use slang to cover up words that might make us uncomfortable. The English language has tons of slang words for violent actions. Get a piece of paper. At the top right three verbs: shoot, hit, and kill. Underneath each, write all of the slang terms you can think of for each word. Was it easy to come up with them? What do you think that says about violence in our lives?

STANDING ASIDE— RIGHT OR WRONG?

During past genocides, many people knew but did nothing. Holocaust survivor Elie Wiesel said in a 1986 speech, "Action is the only remedy to indifference: the most insidious danger of all." Philosophers, however, debate what a person should do during genocide. For example, think about doing nothing. One school of thought might say an individual gets to choose for herself whether to stand aside. Another might agree with Wiesel and insist we must help victims.

Draw a circle on a sheet of paper. Pretend that circle is you. Draw some smaller circles around it with lines to the main circle. In each smaller circle, write one thing you might do if you saw genocide taking place. Doing nothing is an okay answer for our exercise. Then look at each small circle. Think of one positive thing and one negative thing that might happen if you did that thing. Does that make it harder to decide what to do?

WORLD WITHOUT WEAPONS?

In 1968, the TV show *Star Trek* aired an episode about violence. An alien turns all the weapons on the *USS Enterprise* into swords! The crewmembers and their enemies the Klingons fight. They threaten to destroy each other. Then they agree to stop. The alien needs hate to live. When the fighting stops, it flees the ship.

Let's take it one step further. What if an alien made all the weapons on Earth disappear? No firearms. No knives (except to cut food or weeds). Nothing that explodes. No swords, either. Write a one-page story about how the disappearing weapons change your daily life. What might you see and not see as you went through your day? Would you feel safer or less safe? How do you think adults would react? Which skills would we need to develop, if any?

Getting to Forgiveness

Revenge for violence often drives individuals—and groups and nations—to commit violence. To get beyond violence will require human beings to forgive. Forgiving someone for a little thing is hard. How do we forgive for a terrible crime? Or for genocide? Yet Primo Levi, a Holocaust survivor, said, "An enemy who sees the error of his ways ceases to be an enemy."

Sometimes we need a map to get to forgiveness. Think about a time someone hurt you. Now draw a map. It can be of any place. An imaginary place is good, too. Think about what kinds of things keep us from forgiving. Draw each thing you think of as a desert, dragon, volcano—whatever gets in the way of your journey. How would you get past the obstacles on the map? Is it possible to get past obstacles to forgiveness?

TIMELINE

Sun Tzu
The author of *The Art of War* and one of China's most famous philosophers

Xun Kuang
An ancient philosopher who believed humans were born to do evil

Immanuel Kant
A philosopher in the 1700s–1800s who wrote about right and wrong

Mahatma Gandhi
A spiritual leader whose nonviolent protests helped free India from British control

Sophie Scholl
A college student killed for her antiwar beliefs

Hannah Arendt
A philosopher known for her thinking on violence and power

Primo Levi
A Jewish Italian chemist who survived the Holocaust and wrote books on his experiences

Martin Luther King Jr.
A minister whose nonviolent leadership helped African Americans win civil rights

Malcolm X
An African American activist who rejected nonviolent protest

Philippa Foot
The British philosopher who invented the Trolley Problem

GLOSSARY

civil rights
Rights that guarantee all citizens freedom and equality

communist
A system that believes in government control of all parts of society

concentration camps
A place that imprisons large numbers of people from a specific group or groups

controversy
A heated disagreement

ethnicity
To belong to a group that shares a certain culture or birthplace

genre
A category of storytelling with a certain style, form, or content

nurture versus nature
The idea of what we learn (nurture) versus what we're born as (nature)

oppression
Unfair control of one group by a more powerful group

popular culture
Art and entertainment aimed at a large audience

self-defense
Defending yourself against violence by using force

FIND OUT MORE

Clayton, Ed, and Bermudez, Donald. *Martin Luther King: The Peaceful Warrior.* Somerville, MA: 2017.

Freedman, Russell. *We Will Not Be Silent: The White Rose Student Resistance Movement.* New York, Clarion Books, 2016.

Keat, Nawuth, and Kendall, Martha. *Alive in the Killing Fields: Surviving the Khmer Rouge Genocide.* Washington, DC: National Geographic Children's Books, 2009.

WORKS CONSULTED

Arendt, Hannah. *On Violence.* New York: Harcourt, Brace, & World, 1970.

Chavez, Nicole, and Almasy, Steve. "What happened, moment by moment, in the Florida school massacre." CNN.com. Internet. March 8, 2018. https://www.cnn.com/2018/02/15/us/florida-school-shooting-timeline/index.html

Gabbatiss, Josh. "Is violence embedded in our DNA?" Sapiens.org, July 12, 2017. https://www.sapiens.org/evolution/human-violence-evolution/

"Moral philosophy and genocide." Center for Philosophy for Children. Internet. Undated. https://depts.washington.edu/nwcenter/lessonplans/moral-philosophy-and-genocide/

"What is genocide?" United States Holocaust Museum. Internet. Undated. https://www.ushmm.org/wlc/en/article.php?ModuleId=10007043

ON THE INTERNET

"A Class Divided." *Frontline.* Public Broadcasting System. https://www.pbs.org/wgbh/frontline/film/class-divided/

Martin Luther King Jr. Acceptance Speech. *Nobelprize.org.* Nobel Media AB 2014. Internet. Video. https://www.nobelprize.org/mediaplayer/index.php?id=1853

Survivor Testimonies: The United States Holocaust Museum www.ushmm.org/remember/the-holocaust-survivors-and-victims-resource-center/survivors-and-victims/survivor-testimonies

INDEX

Arendt, Hannah	8
chimpanzees	11
Gandhi, Mahatma	7, 21
Genocide	12, 13, 14
Cambodia	15
Darfur,	14, 15
The Holocaust	12, 13, 14
King, Martin Luther	21
Lemkin, Raphael	12, 13
nonviolence	20, 21, 22
oppression	9, 10, 21
pacifism	20, 22
power	8, 18
Scholl, Sophie	22
science	10, 11, 22
self-defense	9, 22
Sun Tzu	7
video games	18
women	5, 9

ABOUT THE AUTHOR

Kevin Cunningham is the author of more than 70 books for children and adults. One of his hobbies is asking big, impossible-to-answer questions. He lives near Chicago, Illinois.